VIOLIN PLAY-ALONG

AUDIO ACCESS INCLUDED

IRISH TUNES

T0081922

CONTENTS

To access audio visit:
www.halleonard.com/mylibrary

Enter Code
3265-6333-1053-8645

ISBN 978-1-61780-774-9

HAL•LEONARD®
CORPORATION
7777 W. BLUEMOUND RD. P.O. BOX 13819 MILWAUKEE, WI 53213

In Australia Contact:
Hal Leonard Australia Pty. Ltd.
4 Lentara Court
Cheltenham, Victoria, 3192 Australia
Email: ausadmin@halleonard.com.au

Recorded and Produced at
Beathouse Music, Milwaukee, WI

Kaitlin Hahn, Fiddle
Randy Gosa, Guitar
John Karr, Bodhran

Visit Hal Leonard Online at
www.halleonard.com

The Irish Washerwoman

Irish Folksong

King of the Fairies

Traditional Irish

The Little Beggarman

Traditional Irish Folk Song

Mason's Apron

Traditional Irish

St. Anne's Reel

Traditional Celtic Folksong

Star of Munster

Traditional Irish

Temperence Reel

Traditional

Lively

The Kesh Jig

Traditional Irish